D0852024

DISCOVERING AMERICA

Northern New England

MAINE • NEW HAMPSHIRE • VERMONT

By
Thomas G. Aylesworth
Virginia L. Aylesworth

CHELSEA HOUSE PUBLISHERS
New York • Philadelphia

First Printing

1   3   5   7   9   8   6   4   2

Library of Congress Cataloging-in-Publication Data

Aylesworth, Thomas G.
    Northern New England: Maine, New Hampshire, Vermont
Thomas G. Aylesworth, Virginia L. Aylesworth.
    p. cm.—(Discovering America)
    Includes bibliographical references and index.
    ISBN 0-7910-3397-X.
        0-7910-3415-1 (pbk.)
    1. New England—Juvenile literature. 2. Maine—Juvenile literature. 3. New Hampshire—
Juvenile literature. 4. Vermont—Juvenile literature. I. Aylesworth, Virginia L. II. Title. III.
Series: Aylesworth, Thomas G. Discovering America.

F4.3.A95   1996   94-42012
974—dc20   CIP
                                            AC

CONTENTS

VERMONT

Maine

The state seal of Maine was adopted in 1820. In the center is a pine tree that is flanked by a farmer and a seaman, representing the two chief occupations of the state. A moose lies at the foot of the tree, and over the tree is the North Star and the state motto, "Dirigo." At the bottom of the seal is the name *Maine*.

State Flag

The state flag of Maine was adopted in 1909 and contains the state seal on a field of blue—the same blue that is found in the flag of the United States.

Maine also has a merchant marine flag. On a field of white, *Dirigo* is written in blue letters. Beneath that is a pine tree around which is twined a blue anchor. Below the tree and anchor is the name *Maine* printed in blue.

State Motto

Dirigo

This motto, which means "I direct" or "I lead" in Latin repeats the idea of the North Star, an important navigational guide, on the state seal.

The Maine coast near Bar Harbor attracts many tourists.

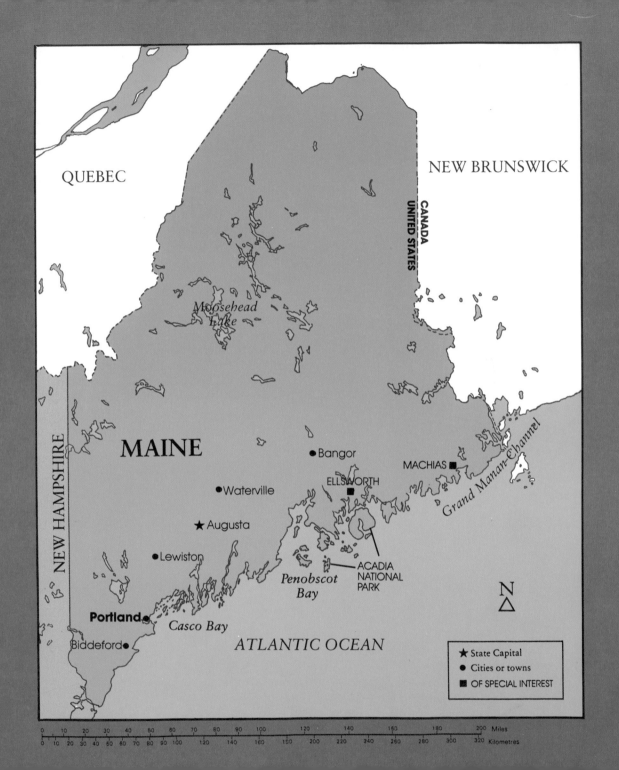

MAINE
At a Glance

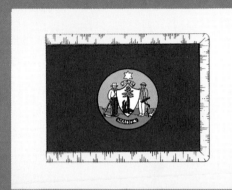

State Flag

Capital: Augusta

Major Industries: Paper and wood products, textiles, fishing

Major Crops: Potatoes, apples, sweet corn, blueberries

State Bird: Chickadee

State Flower: White Pine Cone and Tassel

Size: 33,265 square miles (39th largest)
Population: 1,235,396 (39th largest)

State Name and Nicknames

No one really knows where the name of the state of Maine came from. There are those who think that early French explorers named it after the French province of Maine. On the other hand, *main* was a common word used by explorers to mean "mainland."

Maine is often called the *Pine Tree State*, since pines are so common in its 17 million acres of forests. It is also called the *Lumber State* because of the importance of that industry, and the *Border State* because it is bordered by Canada. Another nickname is *Old Dirigo* because of its motto.

State Capital

When Maine became a state in 1820, the first capital was Portland. In 1832, Augusta became the capital.

State Flower

The cone and tassel of the white pine, *Pinus strobus*, was named the state flower of Maine in 1895.

State Tree

Pinus strobus, the eastern white pine, was named the official tree of Maine in 1959.

State Bird

The chickadee, *Penthestes atricapillus*, became the state bird of Maine in 1927.

State Animal

The moose, *Alces americanus*, was named the state animal of Maine in 1979.

State Cat

In 1985 the Maine coon cat was named state cat.

State Fish

The landlocked salmon, *Salmo salar sebago*, was adopted as the state fish in 1969.

State Fossil

Pertica quadrifaria, an ancient plant, was named the state fossil in 1985.

State Insect

The honeybee, *Apis mellifera*, became the state insect in 1975.

State Mineral

Tourmaline has been the state mineral since 1971.

State Song

"State of Maine Song," with words and music by Roger Vinton Snow, is the official song of the state.

Population

The population of Maine in 1992 was 1,235,396, making it the 39th most populous state. There are 40 people per square mile, and about 97 percent of "Down Easters" were born in the United States.

The Maine coon cat is the state cat.

Although most of the population is of English or Scots-Irish descent, many residents, especially in the northern part of the state, are French Canadians.

Industries

The principal industries of the state are manufacturing, tourism, finance, insurance, and construction. The chief products are paper and wood articles, electrical and electronics products, leather goods, and boats.

Agriculture

The chief crops of the state are potatoes, hay, apples, blueberries, and sweet corn. Maine is also a livestock state, and there are estimated to be some 135,000 cattle; 79,000 hogs and pigs; 17,000 sheep; and 4.9 million chickens, geese, and turkeys on its farms. Pine, spruce, and fir timber are harvested; sand, gravel, and crushed stone are important mineral products. Commercial fishing, including lobstering, brought

A moose in a lake in northern Maine browses on aquatic plants, one of its favorite foods.

in $163.3 million in 1992.

Government

The governor is the only Maine executive elected directly by the people of the state and serves a four-year term. The state legislature, which meets every other year, has a 35-member senate and a 151-member house of representatives. These legislators are elected from each of the state's counties, which send from one to five senators and three to 28 representatives to the capital, depending on the population of the county. The state constitution was adopted in 1819. In addition to its two U.S. senators, Maine has two representatives in the U.S. House of Representatives. The state has four votes in the electoral college.

Sports

Maine's woods, lakes, and rivers have made the state a popular place for hunting and fishing. Downhill and cross-country skiing are popular in the winter. In the summer, many people enjoy cruising the state's extensive coastline in sail or motor boats.

Major Cities

Augusta (population 21,325). Settled in 1628, Augusta is the capital of Maine and is located at the head of navigation on the Kennebec River. It began as a trading post, established by men from the Plymouth Colony on the site of Cushnoc, an Indian village.

In 1754, Fort Western was built to protect the settlers from Indian raids. Today, some of the leading industries in the city are textiles, clothing, steel, and food processing. Things to see in Augusta include the statehouse (1829-32), the State Museum, and Blaine House.

White water rafting on Maine's inland rivers attracts many sports enthusiasts to the state.

Lewiston (population 39,757). Settled in 1770, Lewiston is Maine's second largest city. Located 30 miles up the Androscoggin River from the sea, it is directly across the river from Auburn. A manufacturing town specializing in shoes, textiles, electronics, computers, and metal fabrication, Lewiston is the site of Bates College—New England's first coeducational institution of higher learning. Things to see in Lewiston include Mount David and the Treat Art Gallery.

Portland (population 64,358). Portland, which was settled in 1631, is Maine's largest city and is located on beautiful Casco Bay. It is a city with regal elm trees, stately houses, and historic churches. Before the Revolution, Portland was raided by the Indians several times, and during the war, in 1775, the British bombarded it, later

The old port section of Portland, an area also known as the Old Port Exchange.

burning it down. A fire wiped out large sections of the city in 1866, and poet Henry Wadsworth Longfellow said that the ruined town reminded him of Pompeii (an ancient city in southern Italy that was destroyed and buried by a volcanic eruption).

Things to see in Portland include the Wadsworth-Longfellow House (1785), the Maine Historical Society, the Tate House (1755), Victoria Mansion (1858), the Portland Museum of Art, the Old Port Exchange, Portland Head Light (1791), and the Parson Smith House (1764).

The Portland Head Light is Maine's oldest lighthouse, built in 1791.

Places To Visit

The National Park Service maintains three areas in the state of Maine: Acadia National Park, part of White Mountain National Forest, and Saint Croix Island International Historic Site. In addition, there are 23 state recreation areas.

Auburn: Norlands Living History Center. This center is a village that shows farm life as it was lived a century ago.

Bailey Island: Bailey Island Bridge. This structure is built of uncemented granite rocks that let the tides flow between them.

Bath: Fort Popham Memorial. Here are the remains of an unfinished fort with its gun emplacements. Bath Maritime Museum. The history of Maine's ship building industry and commerce is exhibited in several buildings including a working shipwright's shed.

Bethel: Dr. Moses Mason House. Built in 1813, this house was the home of a congressman who served in the Jackson administration.

Blue Hill: Parson Fisher House. Designed and built in 1814 by the town's first minister, the Parson Fisher House contains his memorabilia.

Boothbay Harbor: Boothbay Railway Village. This village contains two restored railroad stations and an old-fashioned general store.

Brunswick: First Parish Church. This 1846 church contains the family pew of Harriet Beecher Stowe and the pulpit from which Henry Wadsworth Longfellow once spoke. Bowdoin College Museum of Art. The collection includes paintings by Winslow Homer and Andrew Wyeth.

Bucksport: Jed Prouty Tavern. Built in 1792 as a stagecoach stop, the tavern, which is still in operation, played host to Presidents Martin Van Buren, Andrew Jackson, William Henry Harrison, and John Tyler.

Camden: Old Conway House Complex. Here is a restored 18th-century farmstead, complete with farm implements and a blacksmith shop.

Damariscotta: Saint Patrick's Church. Built in 1808, this

The old mill in Brunswick is a reminder of the early nineteenth century, when waterpower made New England the manufacturing center of the United States.

The house in Brunswick where Harriet Beecher Stowe lived with her family while her husband was on the faculty at Bowdoin College.

Montpelier, the reconstructed home of General Henry Knox, in Thomaston.

brick church is the oldest Roman Catholic church in New England.

Farmington: Nordica Homestead. The birthplace of Lillian Nordica, the famous Wagnerian soprano, built in 1840, displays many of her costumes and other memorabilia.

Houlton: Market Square Historic District. The district is made up of a group of buildings dating from ihe 1860s.

Kennebunk: Taylor-Barry House. Built in 1803, the Taylor-Barry House was the home of a sea captain.

Kennebunkport: Seashore Trolley Museum. The museum contains some 150 antique streetcars from the United States and abroad.

Kittery: Sarah Orne Jewett House. Built in 1774, this house was the home of the author of *The Country of the Pointed Firs*.

Lubec: Roosevelt Campobello International Park. Jointly owned by the United States and Canada, this island park was once the summer home of President Franklin D. Roosevelt.

Machias: Ruggles House. This house, built in 1820, features delicately carved woodwork and an unusual "flying" staircase.

Ogunquit: Marginal Way. Marginal Way is a walk along the cliffs overlooking the ocean with tidepools at the water's edge.

Old Town: Old Town Canoe Company. This company is the only remaining production company in the United States making canoes.

Poland Spring: Shaker Museum. This museum consists of six buildings, one of them dating back to 1794, that contain furniture and other artifacts created by the Shakers, a 19th century religious sect.

Rockland: Owls Head Transportation Museum. The museum features working displays of antique cars, airplanes, and a huge steam engine.

Saco: Maine Aquarium. The aquarium contains more than 150 species of marine life, including seals, penguins, eels, sharks, and tropical fish.

Thomaston: Montpelier. Today's Montpelier is a reproduction of the house built by General Henry Knox, the Revolutionary War hero, in 1795.

Wiscasset: Nickels-Sortwell House. Built in 1807 for a sea captain, this house was later used as a hotel from 1820 to 1900. Musical Wonder House-Music Museum. A collection of music boxes and player pianos is displayed in a house built in 1852.

York: York Village. This section of York contains the Old Gaol (1720), the Emerson–Wilcox House (1742), Jefferd's Tavern (1759), The Old School House (1755), the Elizabeth Perkins House (1730), and the John Hancock Warehouse.

A pier in Wiscasset harbor leads to a float that rises and falls with the extreme tides of coastal Maine.

Events

There are many events and organizations that schedule activities of various kinds in the state of Maine. Here are some of them:

Sports: Fishing Tournament (Bailey Island), Kenduskeag Stream Canoe Race (Bangor), harness racing at Bass Park (Bangor), Great Adventures (Bingham), Tuna Tournament (Boothbay Harbor), 'Roostook River Raft Race (Caribou), Winter Sports Events (Fort Kent), Friendship Sloop Races (Friendship), Meduxnekeeg River Canoe Race (Houlton),

In Old Orchard Beach, where an annual art festival is held, the pier and lively boardwalk contribute to the pleasure of vacationers.

Spudland Open Golf Tournament (Presque Isle), Sled Dog Race (Rangeley), Maine Snow-Pro (Scarborough).

Arts and Crafts: Art Exhibit (Bar Harbor), Antique Show (Boothbay Harbor), Quilt Show (Bridgton), Garden Club Open House Day (Camden), Annual Art Festival (Old Orchard Beach), Sidewalk Art Show (Portland), Art Show (York), Antique Show (York), Craft Fair (York).

Music: Band concerts (Bangor), Bangor Symphony (Bangor), Bluegrass Festival (Brunswick), Brunswick Music Theater (Brunswick), Bowdoin Summer Music Festival (Brunswick), New England Music Camp (Waterville), Portland Symphony (Portland), Kotzschmar Memorial Organ Concerts (Portland).

Entertainment: Norlands Special Events (Auburn), Whatever Week (Augusta),

Bangor Fair (Bangor), Belfast Bay Festival (Belfast), Blue Hill Fair (Blue Hill), Fisherman's Festival (Boothbay Harbor), Windjammer Days (Boothbay Harbor), Obsolete Auto Show (Boothbay Harbor), Fall Foliage Festival (Boothbay Harbor), Winter Carnival (Bridgton), Winter Carnival (Caribou), Homecoming Week (Eastport), Franklin County Fair (Farmington), Chester Greenwood Day Celebration

(Farmington), Houlton Potato Feast (Houlton), Franco-American Festival (Lewiston), Indian Pageant (Old Town), Old Port Festival (Portland), Deering Oaks Family Festival (Portland), Northern Maine Fair (Presque Isle), Maine Lobster Festival (Rockland), Transportation Rally (Rockland), Storytellers Festival (Rockport), Skowhegan State Fair (Skowhegan), Skowhegan Log Day (Skowhegan), Clam Festival (Yarmouth).

Theater: Theater Project of Brunswick (Brunswick), Camden Amphitheatre (Camden), Ogunquit Playhouse (Ogunquit), Mad Horse Theater Company (Portland), Portland Stage Company (Portland), Acadia Repertory Company (Somesville).

A lobsterman in Boothbay harbor uses wooden traps not much different from those used in the early days of the colony.

Windjammers, which were important as lumbering ships earlier this century, now often take passengers for cruises of Maine's coastal waters.

The Land

The White Mountains region of Maine covers the northern section of the state. It is in this area that the rugged landscape becomes more heavily forested and dotted with lakes.

Maine is bordered on the west by New Hampshire and the Canadian province of Quebec, on the north by the Canadian provinces of Quebec and New Brunswick, on the east by New Brunswick, and on the south by the Atlantic Ocean. The state has three main land regions: the Coastal Lowlands, the Eastern New England Upland, and the White Mountains Region.

The Coastal Lowlands form a strip along Maine's Atlantic shoreline. They are part of a larger land area that stretches along the entire New England coast. In the south there are broad, sandy beaches that give way to salt marshes. In the north are small bays along a rocky coast dominated by high cliffs. Sand, gravel, granite, and limestone are important mineral resources here. Fishermen and lobstermen sail from ports along the Coastal Lowlands, and farmers raise blueberries, beef cattle, and poultry in the region. Off the coast are thousands of islands, of which the largest is Mount Desert.

The Eastern New England Upland is northwest of the Coastal Lowlands. It is part of a shelflike formation that extends from Canada to Connecticut. In Maine, the area rises to several thousand feet above sea level. The Aroostook Plateau, in the northeast, has rich soil in which the famous Maine potatoes are grown. Dairy and beef cattle thrive here, and forestry is another important industry of the region.

Maine has more than 3,000 miles of coastline. Sea-related industries are very important to the state and fishermen and lobstermen have depended on the ocean for their livelihood for centuries.

The mountainous areas of Maine are a popular attraction for skiing enthusiasts every year.

The White Mountains Region covers northwestern Maine and extends into New Hampshire and Vermont. This mountainous area has hundreds of lakes and a series of eskers, or low gravel ridges formed during the Ice Age. Maine's coastline is 228 miles long. It has over 5,000 rivers and streams and more than 2,500 lakes and ponds. Its highest point is 5,268-foot Mount Katahdin; in central Maine.

Casco Bay, near Portland, is one of the many large bays, coves, and inlets that comprise the state's coastline.

The Climate

Maine's annual precipitation is between 35 and 45 inches, much of it falling as snow during the winter months. Summers are short and relatively cool; winters are cold and long. The coastal areas are relatively temperate, with Portland having an average January temperature of 21 degrees Fahrenheit and an average July temperature of 68 degrees F. Weather changes are often sudden and severe. The northern forests may have winter temperatures below 0 degrees F. and up to 100 inches of snow per year.

The History

Before the arrival of European explorers, thousands of Indians lived in what would become the state of Maine. Most of them belonged to the Algonquian language family. They included the Penobscots, the Passamaquoddies, and the Abnaki tribe, which lived west of the Penobscot River. The Etchemin lived east of the river. Sometimes their villages were raided by Iroquois people from what is now New York state.

There is evidence that the first Europeans to arrive in the Maine area were members of a Viking expedition led by Leif Ericson, who may have landed about A.D. 1000. The next visitor of record was John Cabot, an Italian sea captain in the service of the English, who probably arrived in 1498. Cabot was followed in 1524 by the Italian Giovanni da Verrazano, employed by the French. The Frenchmen Pierre du Guast and Samuel de Champlain both arrived in 1604. Maine's first non-Indian settlement was founded by the French on St. Croix Island in 1604 but it lasted for only one winter.

An Englishman, George Waymouth, explored the Maine coast in 1605 on behalf of two wealthy countrymen, Sir Ferdinando Gorges and Sir John Popham. They were so impressed with Waymouth's description of the area that they sent a group of colonists to the New World in 1607. This group established Popham Plantation near the mouth of the Kennebec River. The settlement lasted only about a year, during which time the colonists built America's first transatlantic trading ship, the *Virginia*. In 1608 cold weather and other hardships forced the settlers to return to England. The British established another colony near present-day Saco in 1623, and others followed later in the decade.

In 1622 Gorges and another Englishman, John Mason, were given a large tract of land by the Council for New England, which was an

Navigator Sebastian Cabot and his father, John Cabot, made landings on the Maine coast in the late 1490s. Italian by birth, they were employed by England to find a sea route to the Indies, and their voyage of 1497 gave England a strong claim to the North American mainland, including what is now Canada. After his father's death, Sebastian Cabot sailed west again in search of a passage across the northern edge of the New World. His explorations resulted in some of the most accurate maps of the 16th century.

agency of the British government. The grant included a large part of what is now Maine and New Hampshire. In 1629 the two men divided the territory, and Gorges took the Maine section. He established a government in 1636, and in 1641 he made the town of Gorgeana (now York) a city—the first chartered English city in what is now the United States.

Gorges died in 1647, and the towns of Kittery, Wells, and York united under a new government. By 1658 these three towns, along with Casco Bay, Kennebunk, Saco, and Scarborough, had joined the Massachusetts Bay Colony. The heirs of Ferdinando Gorges objected that the Maine area was theirs, and in 1664 an English board of commissioners returned Maine to the Gorges family. The dispute was resolved when Massachusetts bought the area from them for about $6,000 in 1677.

Between 1689 and 1763, the French and Indian Wars brought conflict to Maine and all of New England, as the British vied with the French and their Indian allies for the territory. When the wars ended, France gave up its claims to Maine and most of North America to the British.

During the 1760s, the people of Maine and the other colonies objected to taxes and trade restrictions imposed by the British government to pay for the colonial wars. There was even a "York Tea Party" in 1774, when a group of Maine men burned a supply of British tea in that town. When the Revolutionary War began in 1775, hundreds of men from Maine joined the Continental Army. The British retaliated by blocking trade in Maine, which caused a shortage of food and other necessities. The British also burned the town of Falmouth (present-day Portland) in 1775, as punishment for opposition to colonial policy.

The first naval battle of the Revolutionary War was fought off Machias in 1775, when Maine men captured the British ship *Margaretta*. That same year, General Benedict Arnold and his men set out from Augusta to attack Quebec, but they were repulsed by the British. In 1779 British troops took the town of Castine.

French explorer, fur trader, cartographer, and colonizer Samuel de Champlain explored much of the Maine coast early in the 17th century. Champlain founded the city of Quebec in 1608 and laid the foundations for what was called New France (now Canada).

After the war ended in 1783, Massachusetts gave parts of the
Maine area to war veterans in place of back pay, and population
increased. The pine forests were Maine's economic backbone in the
early 1800s: they were used to create a thriving shipbuilding
industry. Trade with other countries flourished until 1807, when the
Embargo Act slowed down the shipping industry but fostered the
growth of manufacturing to offset the economic loss.

After the War of 1812, the movement to separate Maine from
Massachusetts found many supporters. Maine residents voted for
separation in 1819, and in 1820 Maine entered the Union as the
23rd state, with Portland as its capital. Augusta became the capital in
1832. Maine's admission was affected by the Missouri Compromise,
by which Missouri was admitted as a slave state and Maine as a free
state in order to maintain the balance between slave and free states.
In 1842 a long-standing dispute about the Maine boundary with
Canada was resolved by the Webster-Ashburton Treaty.

Anti-slavery feelings were strong in Maine for 30 years before the
Civil War broke out in 1861. Some 72,000 Maine men joined the
Union Army during the conflict, and the nation's vice-president
during Abraham Lincoln's first term was Hannibal Hamlin, who had
served as Maine's governor.

After the war, Maine industry prospered, especially textiles and
leather goods. During the 1890s, the state's many rivers were utilized
for generating hydroelectric power. Throughout the early 1900s, the
number of small farms in the state decreased, and many large farms
were started; they specialized in the cultivation of potatoes and in
dairy and poultry products. Paper and pulp industries began to take
up the industrial slack created by the relocation of many textile
factories to the South, where labor was cheaper.

During the 1940s, one of the best-known political figures in
Washington was a Maine woman, Margaret Chase Smith. She was
the first woman to win election to the House of Representatives and
then to the Senate.

During World War II, about 95,000 men and women from Maine served in the armed forces. Boots, shoes and military uniforms poured from Maine's factories. Cargo and combat ships were built at Bath and South Portland. During the 1950s Air Force bases were constructed in the state, increasing the population of surrounding communities.

Today, Maine continues its economic growth. Industry and agriculture are well balanced, and the state has become a favorite with tourists, who spent $2.75 billion in 1991. Maine is known for having the highest tides, the tastiest potatoes, and the tartest conversations in the country ("Down Easters," as Maine residents are called, are famous for not wasting words). Their nickname probably originated from the early New England use of the word "down" to mean "north."

Much of Portland's economic growth came during World War II when its factories produced uniforms for the war effort. The city is still one of Maine's centers of industry.

Revolutionary War general Henry Knox made his home in Thomaston, in a grand mansion he called Montpelier. As a colonel in the Continental Army, fought under George Washington at the Battle of Trenton (1776) and was promoted to brigadier general. In 1785 he became the nation's first secretary of war.

Education

The first school in Maine may have been at an Indian mission founded in 1696. The first school for settlers opened in York in 1701, but tax-supported schools did not begin until 1868. By the time Maine became a state, it had two institutions of higher education: Bowdoin College (1794) and Colby College (1813). The University of Maine was established in 1865.

Poet Henry Wadsworth Longfellow was born in Portland. He is perhaps best remembered for his verse on Indian life entitled "The Song of Hiawatha". One of his finest poems, "The Cross of Snow," was written as a tribute to his wife 18 years after her accidental death. Longfellow was the first American to be honored in the Poet's Corner of London's Westminster Abbey.

The People

Slightly more than 47 percent of the people of Maine live in towns or cities such as Portland, Lewiston, and Bangor. Most of them were born in the United States. The largest single religious denomination is the Roman Catholic, but there are more Protestants than Catholics in Maine, most of them Baptists, Episcopalians, Methodists, and members of the United Church of Christ.

Many famous people were born in the state of Maine. The following are some of the more notable figures.

Hampden native Dorothea Dix began a nationwide campaign to improve conditions for prisoners, the mentally retarded, and the mentally ill in 1841. Advocating a humane approach to the treatment of mental illness, she was instrumental in establishing more than 30 health care facilities.

Stephen King, a writer of best-selling horror novels.

Publishers and Journalists
Cyrus Curtis 1850-1933, Portland. Founder of Curtis Publishing Company

George Palmer Putnam 1814-72, Brunswick. Founder of G. P. Putnam & Sons publishing house

Inventors
Hiram Stevens Maxim 1840-1916, Sangerville. Inventor of the automatic gun, later named the Maxim gun

Francis Stanley 1849-1918, Kingfield. Co-inventor of the Stanley Steamer automobile

Freelan Stanley 1849-1940, Kingfield. Co-inventor of the Stanley Steamer automobile

Religious Leader
Ellen Gould White 1827-1915, Gorham. Leader of the Seventh-Day Adventists

Government Officials
William Cohen b.1940, Bangor. United States senator

Melville Weston Fuller 1833-1910, Augusta. Chief Justice

Nelson Rockefeller, long-time governor of New York State, served as vice-president under Gerald Ford.

Margaret Chase Smith was the first woman to be elected to the U.S. Senate.

of the United States Supreme Court

Hannibal Hamlin 1809-91, Paris Hill. Vice-president under Lincoln

Rufus King 1755-1857, Scarborough, Mass. (Now in Maine). United States senator and ambassador to Great Britain

Edmund Muskie b.1914, Rumford. Governor, United States senator, Secretary of State

Nelson Rockefeller 1908-79, Bar Harbor. Governor of New York and vice-president under Gerald Ford

Margaret Chase Smith b.1897, Skowhegan. United States senator

Military Figures

Oliver Otis Howard 1830-1909, Leeds. Civil War general and founder of Howard University

William Whipple 1730-85, Kittery. Revolutionary War leader and signer of the Declaration of Independence

Social Reformer

Dorothea Dix 1802-87, Hampden. Pioneer in specialized treatment of the mentally ill

Business Leaders

Charles A. Coffin 1844-1926, Somerset County. Founder of General Electric

William D. Washburn 1831-1912, Livermore. Founded Pillsbury Mills

Entertainer

Linda Lavin b.1937, Portland. Television actress: *Alice*

Director

John Ford 1895-1973, Cape Elizabeth. Five-time Academy Award-winning director: *The Quiet Man*

Writers

Walter Van Tilburg Clark 1909-71, East Orland. Novelist: *The Ox-Bow Incident*

Tristram Coffin 1892-1955, Brunswick. Pulitzer Prize-winning poet: *Strange Holiness*

Sarah Orne Jewett 1849-1909, South Berwick. Novelist: *The Country of the Pointed Firs*

Stephen King b.1947, Portland. Novelist: *The Shining*

Henry Wadsworth Longfellow 1807-82, Portland. Poet: "Paul Revere's Ride"

Edna St. Vincent Millay
1892-1950, Rockland.
Pulitzer Prize-winning
poet: *The Harp Weaver
and Other Poems*

Kenneth Roberts 1885-1957,
Kennebunk. Pulitzer
Prize-winning novelist:
Northwest Passage

**Edward Arlington
Robinson** 1869-1935,
Head Tide. Three-time
Pulitzer Prize-winning
poet: *Tristram*

Colleges and Universities
There are many colleges
and universities in Maine.
Here are the most
prominent, with their
locations, dates of founding,
and enrollments.

Bates College, Lewiston, 1855,
1,515

Bowdoin College, Brunswick,
1794, 1,445

Colby College, Waterville, 1813,
1,716

Saint Joseph's College, Standish,
1912, 819

University of Maine, Orono,
1865, 12,313; *at Augusta,*
1965, 3,525; *at Farmington,*
1864, 2,267; *at Fort Kent,*
1878, 641; *at Machias,* 1909,
958; *at Presque Isle,* 1904,
1,577

**Where To Get More
Information**
Chamber of Commerce
and Industry
126 Sewall Street
Augusta, ME 04330

1-800-533-9595, out-of-state
and during the winter
1-207-623-0363, year-round

New Hampshire

The first seal of New Hampshire was adopted in 1784, and was modified in 1931. The seal is circular, on a blue background. In the center is a reproduction of the Revolutionary War frigate *Raleigh*, surrounded by laurel to symbolize victory. Around the center is printed "Seal of the State of New Hampshire" with the date "1776," the year the state's first constitution was adopted. The outside ring of the seal contains nine laurel leaves alternating with stars.

New Hampshire also has a state emblem, adopted in 1945 and amended in 1957. The emblem is oval and contains a drawing of the Old Man of the Mountain (a rock formation in Franconia Notch State Park). Surrounding the drawing is the state motto at the bottom and the words *New Hampshire* at the top.

State Flag

The state flag, adopted in 1909 and modified in 1931, shows the state seal on a blue background.

State Motto

Live Free or Die

Adopted by the state legislature in 1945, these words were spoken by General John Stark as a toast at a veterans' reunion on July 31, 1809.

Scenic Newfound Lake in Bristol, New Hampshire.

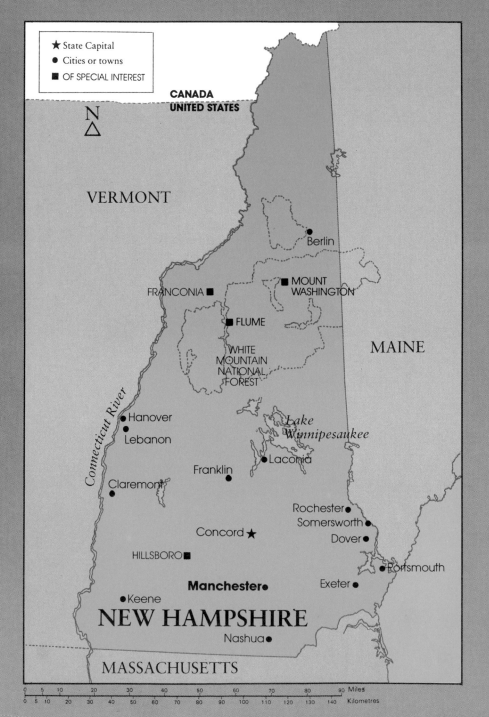

N

CANADA
UNITED STATES

VERMONT

Berlin

FRANCONIA ■

■ MOUNT WASHINGTON

■ FLUME

WHITE MOUNTAIN NATIONAL FOREST

MAINE

Connecticut River

Hanover
Lebanon

Lake Winnipesaukee

Laconia

Franklin

Claremont

Rochester
Somersworth
Dover

Concord ★

HILLSBORO ■

Portsmouth

Manchester ●

Exeter

Keene

NEW HAMPSHIRE

Nashua ●

MASSACHUSETTS

0   5   10   20   30   40   50   60   70   80   90   Miles
0   5   10   20   30   40   50   60   70   80   90 100 110 120 130 140   Kilometres

State Bird: Purple Finch

State Flower: Purple Lilac

NEW HAMPSHIRE
At a Glance

Capital: Concord

State Flag

Size: 9,279 square miles (44th largest)
Population: 1,110,801 (41st largest)

Major Industries: Machinery, computers, forest products, tourism

Major Crops: Dairy products, hay, vegetables, apples, maple syrup

State Name and Nicknames

England gave a grant to Captain John Mason of the Royal Navy in 1629, entitling him to a part of the New World that included what was to become the state of New Hampshire. Mason named the area for the British county of Hampshire, where he lived for much of his youth.

New Hampshire was nicknamed the *Granite State* because of the huge number of granite formations and quarries. It is also called the *White Mountain State* for the beautiful mountain range in the northern part of the state. The mountains also gave it another name, the *Switzerland of America*. The many rivers flowing from these mountains gave it yet another name, *The Mother of Rivers*.

State Capital

Before New Hampshire became a state, the capital was first Portsmouth (1679-1774), then Exeter (1775-81), and finally Concord (1782-84). For the next several years the capital was in dispute, but Concord was finally selected as the permanent capital in 1808.

State Flower

The purple lilac, *Syringa vulgaris*, was adopted by the legislature in 1919 after a long argument—the Senate wanting the purple aster and the House wanting the apple blossom. Finally, the purple lilac became the compromise choice.

State Tree

In 1947 the white birch, *Betula papyrifera*, was named the state tree at the urging of the New Hampshire Federation of Garden Clubs. This is the tree whose bark was used by the Indians to make their canoes, and it is found in huge numbers all over the state.

State Bird

Even though there were those who preferred the New Hampshire hen, the purple finch, *Carpodacus purpureus*, was named the state bird by the legislature in 1957.

The white birch is the state tree.

State Animal

Common to New Hampshire, the white-tailed deer, *Odocoileus virginianus*, was named the state animal in 1983.

State Insect

The lady bug, *Adalia bipunctata,* was adopted as the state insect in 1977.

State Song

New Hampshire has two state songs. "Old New Hampshire," with words by Dr. John F. Holmes and music by Maurice Hoffman, was adopted by the state legislature in 1949. In 1963 "New Hampshire, My New Hampshire" was added. This song has music by Walter P. Smith and words by Julius Richelson.

Population

The population of New Hampshire in 1992 was 1,110,801, making it the 41st most populous state. There are 123.8 people per square mile. About 3.7 percent of New Hampshirites were born in a foreign country.

Industries

The principal industries of the state of New Hampshire are manufacturing, agriculture, and mining.

The chief products are machinery, electrical and electronic products, plastics, fabricated metal products, and leather goods.

Agriculture

The chief crops of the state are dairy products, eggs, nursery and greenhouse products, hay, vegetables, fruit, maple syrup, and maple sugar products. New Hampshire is also a livestock state, and there are estimated to be some 55,000 cattle; 15,000 horses; 9,500 hogs and pigs; 9,000 sheep; and 310,000 chickens, geese, and turkeys on its farms. Sand, gravel, and stone are important mineral products. Commercial fishing earned $11.5 million in 1992.

Government

The governor is elected for a two-year term. There is no lieutenant governor. The state legislature, called the General Court, which meets every other year, has a senate of 24 members and a house of representatives of no less than 375 and no more than 400 members. These legislators are elected from the state's towns and wards (divisions of cities), which send from one to six legislators to the capital, depending on their populations. The state constitution was adopted in 1784. In addition to its two U.S. senators, New Hampshire has two representatives in the U.S. House of Representatives. The state has four votes in the electoral college.

The purple finch is the state bird.

Major Cities

Concord (population 36,006). Settled in 1727, Concord became the state capital in 1808. It is the financial and political center of the state and also has much diversified industry. The legislature of New Hampshire is the largest in the United States. The state house contains portraits of famous people from New Hampshire. Visitors can also tour the New Hampshire Historical Society, the League of New Hampshire Craftsmen, the Pierce Manse and the Shaker Village in nearby Canterbury.

Manchester (population 99,332). Settled in 1722 Manchester was an industrial center in New Hampshire early on. But when its cotton textile industry failed in 1935, several New Hampshire citizens bought the plants, and this revived the town. Today the city has some 200 industries. Places to visit in Manchester include the Currier Gallery of Art, the Manchester Historic Association, and the McIntyre Ski Area.

Nashua (population 79,662). Settled in 1656, Nashua began as a fur-trading post. Early in the 19th century, the development of Merrimack River waterpower enabled Nashua to become an industrial center. Today this second largest city in the state has more than 100 industries ranging from computers and tools to beer. Travelers can visit Silver Lake State Park and the Nashua Center for the Arts and can tour the Anheuser-Busch Brewery, with its Clydesdale Hamlet in nearby Merrimack.

Places To Visit

The National Park Service maintains two areas in the state of New Hampshire: Saint-Gaudens National Historic Site and White

Sugar maples are tapped for syrup in the early spring.

Sports

Like the other New England states, New Hampshire is known for its ski areas, especially those in the White Mountains. There is sailing on the coast and inland lakes. Fishing and hunting are also popular.

Mountain National Forest. In addition, there are 31 state recreation areas.

Claremont: Fort at N. 4. The Fort at N. 4. is a reconstruction of a fort used by colonists for defense in the French and Indian Wars.

Colebrook: Shrine of Our Lady of Grace. This 25-acre tract contains more than 50 Carrara marble and granite devotional monuments.

Cornish: Saint-Gaudens National Historic Site. Aspet was the home of the sculptor Augustus Saint-Gaudens and displays some of his work.

Dixville Notch: Table Rock. From this rock can be seen parts of New Hampshire, Maine, Vermont, and the Canadian province of Quebec.

Dover: Woodman Institute. This collection of museums includes the Dame Garrison House (1675) and the Woodman House (1818), now a natural history museum.

Exeter: Gillman Garrison House. This house is a renovated garrison (fortified against attack) house of log construction dating from 1690, with an 18th century wing.

Skiing has been a popular winter sport in New Hampshire since 1882, when the first U.S. ski club was founded in Berlin.

The Currier Gallery of Art in Manchester has one of the state's finest art collections.

Franconia: Frost Place. Visitors can see two furnished rooms in the house of the poet Robert Frost.

Franconia Notch State Park: Old Man of the Mountain. This natural formation in the White Mountains is a craggy granite likeness of a man's face, made famous in Nathaniel Hawthorne's short story "The Great Stone Face."

Franklin: Daniel Webster Birthplace. In this frame house, now restored, the statesman Daniel Webster was born in 1782.

Hanover: Dartmouth College. The Dartmouth campus has many fine white brick buildings, some of which date from 1784, also the Baker Memorial Library and the Hopkins Center for the Arts.

Hillsboro: Franklin Pierce Homestead. Built in 1804, this house is the restored childhood home of our 14th President.

Jackson: Heritage-New Hampshire. Thirty theatrical sets, with animation, sounds, and smells, illustrate 300 years of New Hampshire history.

Jefferson: Six Gun City. This is a Western frontier village with rides, a fort, an Indian village, and many other structures.

Keene: Wyman Tavern. Refurnished in 1820s style, the tavern was built in 1762.

Meredith: Winnipesaukee Railroad. The visitor can take scenic train rides in old railroad coaches along the shore of Lake Winnipesaukee.

Mount Washington: Cog railway. Visitors can ride up the west slope of the highest peak in the state.

Peterborough: Peterborough Toy Museum. This fine collection displays many types of antique toys.

Portsmouth: Strawbery Banke. This collection of 37 historic structures displays the history of Portsmouth from 1695 to 1945.

Rindge: Cathedral of the Pines. The Altar of the Nation in this international nondenominational shrine has been recognized by Congress as a memorial to all American war dead.

Events

There are many events and organizations that schedule activities of various kinds in the state of New Hampshire. Here are some of them.

Sports: Winter Carnival (Franklin), Yankee International Racing Federation of America, Inc. Regatta (Littleton), Winterfest (North Conway), Mountainfest (North Conway), Mount Washington Valley Equine Classic (North Conway), Mud Bowl (North Conway), Winter Carnival (Wolfeboro).

Arts and Crafts: Lakes Region Fine Arts and Crafts Festival (Meredith), Craftsmen's Fair (Sunapee).

Music: Band concerts (Hampton Beach), New Hampshire Music Festival (Laconia), New Hampshire Music Festival (Plymouth), Jazz Festival (Portsmouth), Prescott Park Arts Festival (Portsmouth), Festival of the Arts (Waterville Valley).

Entertainment: Lancaster Fair (Jefferson), Cheshire Fair (Kenne), SummerStreet (Littleton), Peterborough Festival Days (Peterborough), Plymouth State Fair (Plymouth), Rochester Fair (Rochester).

Tours: Tours of Dartmouth College (Hanover), InSight Tours (Portsmouth).

Theater: Hampton Playhouse (Hampton Beach), The Old Homestead (Keene), American Stage Festival (Nashua), Barn Playhouse (New London), Eastern Slope Playhouse (North Conway), Weathervane Theatre (Whitefield).

Mount Washington in New Hampshire is the highest peak in the northeastern United States.

An idyllic New England scene right out of a Robert Frost poem. New Hampshire has a wealth of orchards, fruit and vegetable farms, and dairy and poultry farms. The state's

lush woods are brimming with spruce, fir, maple, and birch trees, which contribute to maple syrup, lumber, and paper production—and which provide breathtaking vistas of colorful fall foliage. There is a beautiful stretch of beaches in the southeastern corner, and 72-square-mile Lake Winnipesaukee is only one of many scenic lakes inland. Further north, the majestic White Mountains dominate the landscape.

Squam Lake is in central New Hampshire. New Hampshire contains some 1,300 lakes and ponds, most of them created by the glacial activity of the Ice Age.

The Land

New Hampshire is bounded on the west by Vermont and the Canadian province of Quebec, on the north by Quebec, on the east by Maine and the Atlantic Ocean, and on the south by Massachusetts. The state has three main land regions: the Coastal Lowlands, the Eastern New England Upland, and the White Mountains Region.

Autumn brings magnificently colored foliage to the New Hampshire landscape. Forests cover some 80 percent of the state, and the changing color of their leaves attracts many visitors to see the bright yellows, reds, and oranges cover the hills and valleys.

The rugged terrain of the White Mountains provide exciting campsites for those who enjoy the outdoors.

New Hampshire has the harsh winters typical of northern New England. In the Mount Washington area, a season's snowfall of more than 12 feet is not uncommon.

The Coastal Lowlands are in southeastern New Hampshire, along the Atlantic Ocean. They are part of a larger region that follows the coast of the New England states and extends 15 to 20 miles inland. This is an area of fine beaches and abundant marine life, where fishermen operate their fleets. It also has poultry farms, orchards, and nurseries that grow ornamental plants for market.

The Eastern New England Upland covers the rest of southern New Hampshire from east to west and is part of the same hilly region that extends from northern Maine to eastern Connecticut. The Merrimack Valley, the Hills and Lakes Area, and the New Hampshire part of the Connecticut River Valley are in this region. Mills and factories operate here, as well as hay and fruit farms. Granite, sand, gravel, and mica are quarried in the region. Dairy cows and other livestock contribute to New Hampshire's economy.

The White Mountains region occupies northern New Hampshire. These mountains surround wide, flat areas of spruce, fir, and yellow birch forests. Lumbering and paper manufacturing industries and dairy and potato farms thrive in New Hampshire.

The Climate

The climate of New Hampshire provides relatively short, cool summers and long, severe winters, with up to 150 inches of snow in the mountains. Several slopes in northern New Hampshire provide good spring skiing into April. Annual rainfall ranges from 50 inches in the mountains to about 35 inches near the coast. Concord, the capital, in the southeast, has an average January temperature of 22 degrees Fahrenheit and a July average of 70 degrees F. But in Berlin, in the northern mountains, the average January temperature is 14 degrees F. and the average July temperature is 66 degrees F.

The History

Before the arrival of European explorers, there were probably about 5,000 Indians living in what would become New Hampshire, primarily Abnaki and Pennacook groups whose members spoke Algonquian languages. The Abnaki group included the Ossipee and the Pequawket tribes. In the Pennacook group were the Amoskeag, Nashua, Piscataqua, Souhegan, and Squamscot tribes. All of them were hunters, fishermen, and farmers. They lived in wigwams made of bark and skins, and moved to new locations when fish and game grew scarce.

An Englishman named Martin Pring is the first European known to have explored any part of New Hampshire. He reached the coast in 1603 and sailed up the Piscataqua River, perhaps landing at what is now Portsmouth. In 1605 came the Frenchman Samuel de Champlain, followed by the English captain John Smith, who landed in 1614 on the Isles of Shoals, which he named Smith's Islands.

King James I of England founded a Council for New England in 1620 to encourage settlement in the New World. David Thompson and a small group of colonists were granted lands in present-day New Hampshire, and they arrived near what is now Portsmouth in 1623. They founded a settlement called Odiorne's Point, which is now a part of Rye. At about the same time, another group led by Edward Hilton settled Hilton's Point (now Dover). John Mason named his large land grant between the Merrimack and Piscataqua rivers New Hampshire, for his Hampshire County birthplace in England. Towns sprang up in the area, chiefly along rivers, whose falls provided power for grain mills and sawmills that cut up the fine timber.

New Hampshire was made part of Massachusetts in 1641, but in 1680 Charles II made it a separate colony. During the French and Indian Wars, between 1689 and 1763, the British fought the French

The English explorer Captain John Smith spent several years traveling uncharted areas of New England after he helped found the colony of Jamestown, Virginia, in 1607. In 1614 he landed on New Hampshire's Isles of Shoals and renamed them Smith's Islands. His book *A Description of New England* guided the Pilgrims to Massachusetts.

and their Indian allies, and several New Hampshire colonists won renown as military leaders. Robert Rogers and John Stark helped defeat French invasions from Canada.

The citizens of New Hampshire, like the other colonists, became resentful of the restrictive trade policies and taxes imposed by England during the 1760s. Indeed, the Provincial Congress adopted a constitution making New Hampshire an independent colony in January 1776, six months before the Declaration of Independence was adopted. One of the first armed actions against the British occurred in New Hamsphire in 1774, when John Sullivan led a band of colonists in seizing British military supplies from a fort in New Castle.

When the Revolutionary War broke out in Massachusetts in 1775, hundreds of New Hampshire militiamen rushed to Boston to take part in the fighting. Although New Hampshire was the only one of the 13 original colonies not invaded by the British, its men fought for eight

American naval officer and Revolutionary War hero John Paul Jones was one of New Hampshire's best-known residents during the 18th century. Jones, who lived in Portsmouth, is remembered for his determined response to a British demand to surrender during a naval engagement: "I have not yet begun to fight."

years on land and sea to bring about the victory. In 1788 New Hampshire became the ninth state to ratify the new Constitution of the United States.

After the Revolution, industry and trade became more important in New Hampshire. Ocean commerce on swift clipper ships and commercial fishing flourished. The first railroad was built in 1838. The 1850s brought hosiery plants, woolen mills, and factories that turned out boots, shoes, machine tools, and wood products.

Until the mid-1800s, almost everyone in New Hampshire was of British-colonial stock. Except for those towns with Indian names, most communities had names borrowed from England: Plymouth, Bristol, Concord, Manchester, Colebrook, Bath, Albany, and many more. But when the industrial boom began, a flood of French Canadians arrived to work in the factories.

New Hampshire was a hotbed of abolitionism before the Civil War. Anti-slavery sentiment was one of the factors that sent some 34,000 men from the state into service with Union forces. The Portsmouth Naval Yard turned out many blockade ships for the U.S. Navy between 1861 and 1865. After the war, the state's industrial growth continued, although agriculture remained important.

A view of Concord in 1852. In the mid-19th century, New Hampshire embarked upon a new era of industrial expansion.

55

Dartmouth College, New Hampshire's first college, was established in Hanover in 1769. In 1816 the college became the focus of a famous legal battle called the Dartmouth College Case. The conflict centered around the state's desire to take control of the college and to rename it Dartmouth University. Alumnus Daniel Webster argued the case for Dartmouth and won. The ruling, important in legal history, helped to establish the inviolability of contracts.

During World War I, which the United States entered in 1917, the Portsmouth Naval Yard produced many warships, and some 20,000 New Hampshire men served in the armed forces during the conflict. In the following decade, the cotton and woolen industries declined, due to cheaper labor in Southern mills, and leather and shoe manufacturing became the state's leading industries. New roads and hydroelectric plants were built.

Some 60,000 New Hampshire men and women served in the armed forces during World War II, and Portsmouth retained its status as a major New England port and shipbuilder during the years 1941 to 1945. The mills made thousands of military uniforms under government contracts to wartime industries.

Today, many segments of New Hampshire's economy are still growing. Electronics and precision instruments are among the newer industries, and tourism accounts for more than $4 billion in annual revenue. The state's beautiful beaches, mountains, and ski resorts attract visitors from all over the Northeast.

Education

   Some of the one-room schoolhouses established by early settlers still stand in New Hampshire. The first public-education laws were passed in 1789, and the state's first free library opened at Peterborough in 1833. New Hampshire's first institution of higher education was Dartmouth College, founded in 1769. The University of New Hampshire, established in 1866, was the second.

Far left:
Shakers, also called The United Society of Believers in Christ's Second Appearing, have been present in New Hampshire for about 200 years. The religious group derives its name from the "shaking and quaking" that accompanies revelations and spiritual experiences. Shaker Village, in Canterbury, offers visitors an opportunity to explore a traditional Shaker community.

At left:
Traditional craftsmanship is still valued in New Hampshire. The state's many arts-and-crafts fairs are popular events.

Daniel Webster, born in Salisbury in 1782, was a renowned politician, diplomat, and lawyer of the early 19th century. One of the nation's ablest statesmen, he delivered stirring addresses that emphasized the power of the federal government over that of the individual states.

Journalist and social reform advocate Horace Greeley was born in Amherst in 1811. As publisher of the *New York Tribune*, Greeley advocated land reform and protective tariffs and opposed slavery. He popularized the slogan "Go west, young man."

The People

More than 52 percent of the people in New Hampshire live in towns and cities such as Manchester, Nashua, and Concord. Most of them were born in the United States. The largest single religious body is the Roman Catholic Church. There are, however, more Protestants than Catholics in New Hampshire, including Baptists, Episcopalians, Methodists, Unitarian Universalists, and members of the United Church of Christ.

Franklin Pierce, the 14th president of the United States, was born in Hillsboro in 1804. During Pierce's tenure in the White House, the United States signed a trade treaty with Japan, purchased land on the Mexican border, and passed the Kansas-Nebraska Act, by which settlers in these two territories would decide for themselves whether to permit slavery.

Famous People

Many famous people were born in the state of New Hampshire. Here are a few:

Writers

Thomas Bailey Aldrich 1836-1907, Portsmouth. Editor and writer: *The Story of a Bad Boy*

John Irving b.1942, Exeter. Novelist: *The World According to Garp*

Grace Metalious 1924-64, Manchester. Novelist: *Peyton Place*

Architect

Ralph Adams Cram 1863-1942, Hampton Falls. Architect and medieval revivalist.

Artist

Daniel Chester French 1850-1931, Exeter. Sculptor

Publishers and Journalists

Harry Chandler 1864-1944, Landaff. *Los Angeles Times* publisher

Horace Greeley 1811-72,

John Irving is the best-selling author of The World According to Garp.

Amherst. Abolitionist editor of the New York *Tribune*

Sarah Josepha Hale 1788-1879, Newport. Magazine editor and children's poet: ''Mary Had a Little Lamb''

Philosopher and Religious Leader

Mary Baker Eddy 1821-1910, Bow. Founder of Christian Science

Explorer

Alan Shepard b.1923, East Derry. First U.S. astronaut to travel in space

Government Officials

Lewis Cass 1782-1866, Exeter. United States Senator

Salmon P. Chase 1808-73, Cornish. Secretary of the Treasury under Lincoln

Mary Baker Eddy founded the First Church of Christ Scientist.

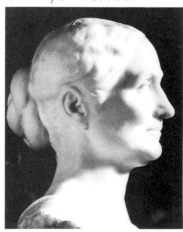

William Pitt Fessenden 1806-69, Boscawen. One of the founders of the Republican party

Franklin Pierce 1804-69, Hillsboro. Fourteenth President of the United States

John Parker Hale Rochester 1806-73, Rochester. United States Senator and Representative and strong opponent of slavery

Harlan Fiske Stone 1872-1946, Chesterfield. Chief Justice of the United States

Daniel Webster 1782-1852, Salisbury. United States senator and famed orator

Henry Wilson 1812-75, Farmington. United States Vice President

Levi Woodbury 1789-1851, Francestown. United States senator and Supreme Court Justice

Military Figures
Benjamin Franklin Butler 1818-93, Deerfield. Union Army general

Fitz-John Porter 1822-1901, Portsmouth. Union Army general

Robert Rogers 1727-95, Dunbarton. Colonial officer in the French and Indian Wars

John Stark 1728-1822, Londonderry. Revolutionary War general

Leonard Wood 1860-1927, Winchester. U.S. Army general and governor-general of the Philippines

Social Reformer
Elizabeth Gurley Flynn 1890-1964, Concord. U.S. Communist leader

Business Leaders
George H. Bissell 1821-84, Hanover. Organizer of the first oil company, The Pennsylvania Rock Oil Co.

Salmon P. Chase, who served as Secretary of the Treasury, appears on the $10,000 bill.

William P. Cheney 1815-95, Hillsboro. Founder of the American Express Company

Ralph S. Damon 1897-1956, Franklin. President of TWA (Transworld Airlines)

John G. Shedd 1850-1926, Alstead. President of Marshall Field & Company

Sports Personality
Jane Blalock b.1945, Portsmouth. Championship golfer

Colleges and Universities
There are several colleges and universities in New Hampshire. Here are the most prominent, with their locations, dates of founding, and enrollment.

Colby-Sawyer College, New London, 1837, 650

Dartmouth College, Hanover, 1769, 5,475

Keene State College, Keene, 1909, 3,987

New England College, Henniker, 1946, 1,062

New Hampshire College, Manchester, 1932, 1,182

Plymouth State College of the University System of New Hampshire, Plymouth, 1871, 4,000

Rivier College, Nashua, 1933, 2,765

Saint Anselm College, Manchester, 1889, 1,857

University of New Hampshire, Durham, 1866, 12,257

Where To Get More Information
New Hampshire Vacation Center
105 Loudon Road
P.O. Box 856
Concord, NH 03301
       or
Department of Resources and Economic Development
New Hampshire Division of Travel & Tourism Development
PO Box 856
Concord, NH 03302-0856
603-271-2666

Vermont

The original state seal was designed in 1779, but fell into disuse. Several other seals were used until 1937, when a modification of the original was adopted. Vermont's state seal is circular and is gold in color. In the center top is a pine tree with 14 branches, representing the original 13 states and Vermont. There are wavy lines at the top representing the sky and wavy lines at the bottom that stand for the sea. On the right of the tree is a cow representing dairying, and at the top of the tree, to the left and right, are sheaves of wheat, representing farming. Slightly below the center of the seal is the word *Vermont* and below that is the state motto: *"Freedom and Unity."*

Historic Groton, Vermont, lies in the foothills of the Green Mountains.

State Flag

The state flag, adopted in 1923, replaced previous state flags of 1803 and 1837. The coat of arms is centered on a blue background.

State Motto

Freedom and Unity

The motto first appeared on the state seal and indicated that the state should be free but united with the other members of the Union.

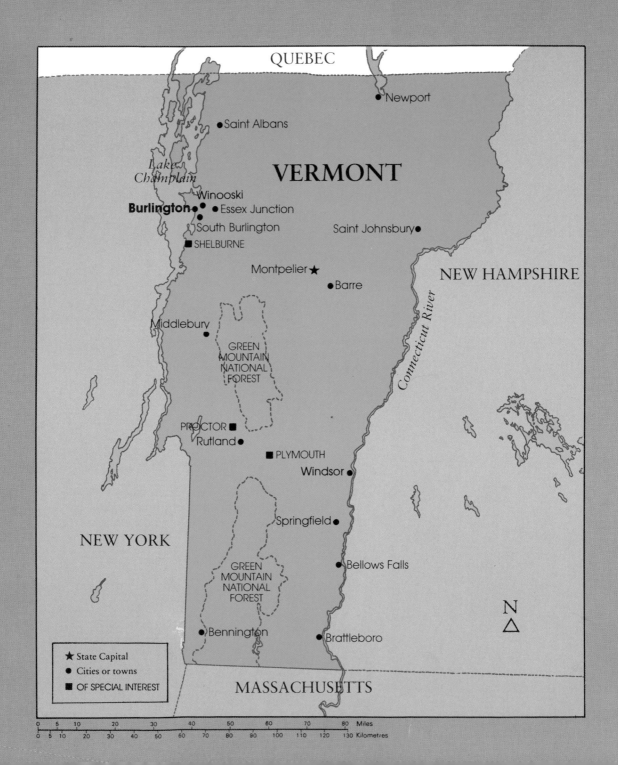

QUEBEC

● Newport

● Saint Albans

*Lake
Champlain*

VERMONT

Winooski
● Essex Junction
Burlington ●
● South Burlington

Saint Johnsbury ●

■ SHELBURNE

NEW HAMPSHIRE

Montpelier ★
● Barre

Middlebury
●

GREEN
MOUNTAIN
NATIONAL
FOREST

Connecticut River

PROCTOR ■
Rutland ●

■ PLYMOUTH

Windsor ●

Springfield ●

NEW YORK

GREEN
MOUNTAIN
NATIONAL
FOREST

Bellows Falls ●

N
△

● Bennington

● Brattleboro

★ State Capital
● Cities or towns
■ OF SPECIAL INTEREST

MASSACHUSETTS

0 5 10   20   30   40   50   60   70   80   Miles
0 5 10   20   30   40   50   60   70   80   90   100   110   120   130 Kilometres

VERMONT
At a Glance

State Flag

Capital: Montpelier

Major Industries: Machine tools, furniture, stone quarrying, agriculture

Major Crops: Apples, maple syrup, hay

State Bird: Hermit Thrush

State Flower: Red Clover

Size: 614 square miles (43rd largest)
Population: 569,784 (49th largest)

State Name and Nickname
   The French explorer Samuel de Champlain named the area *Vert Mont*, or "Green Mountain," on his map of 1647. These same Green Mountains gave the state the nickname of the *Green Mountain State*.

State Capital
   Several towns served as the capital of Vermont before 1808, when Montpelier was selected to be the seat of government.

State Flower
   Trifolium pratense, the red clover, was adopted as the Vermont state flower in 1894.

State Tree
   The sugar maple, *Acer saccharum*, was selected as the state tree in 1949.

State Bird
   Hylocichla guttata, the hermit thrush, was named the state bird in 1941.

The Hermit Thrush, state bird.

State Animal
   In 1961, the Morgan horse was adopted as the state animal of Vermont.

State Beverage
   The state beverage of this dairy state is milk—selected in 1983.

State Fish
   The brook trout is the state cold water fish. The walleye pike has been designated the state warm water fish.

State Insect
   Apis mellifera, the honeybee, was named state insect in 1977.

State Soil
   The state soil of Vermont is the Tunbridge soil series— adopted in 1985.

State Song
   In 1938 "Hail, Vermont" was selected as the state song by a committee that weeded through more than 100 song submissions. The song was written by Josephine Hovey Perry.

Morgan horses are known for both their strength and speed.

Population

The population of Vermont in 1992 was 569,784, making it the 49th most populous state. There are 61.6 persons per square mile—34 percent of them living in towns and cities.

Approximately 97 percent of Vermonters were born in the United States, and more than half of the foreign-born were born in Canada.

Industries

The principal industries of the state of Vermont are manufacturing, agriculture, tourism, trade, and mining. The chief manufactured products are machine tools, furniture, scales, books, computer components, and fishing rods. In 1990, tourists spent $1.25 billion in Vermont.

Agriculture

The chief crops of the state are apples, silage corn, and hay. Agricultural products include maple sugar and

Camel's Hump is one of the highest elevations in the Green Mountains at 4,083 feet.

Hay is one of Vermont's chief crops, important for the dairy industry.

syrup and dairy products. Vermont is also a livestock state, and there are estimated to be 320,000 cattle; 5,100 hogs and pigs; 20,456 sheep; and 406,000 chickens, geese, and turkeys on its farms. Pine, spruce, fir, and hemlock lumber are harvested, and stone, including granite and marble, construction sand, and gravel are important mineral resources.

Government

The governor of Vermont is elected to a two-year term, as are the lieutenant governor, the attorney general, the auditor, the secretary of state, and the treasurer. The state legislature, called the general assembly, which meets in odd-numbered years, has a senate of 30 members and a house of representatives of 150 members. One to six state senators are elected in 12 senatorial districts, depending on population. The state representatives are elected from 72 districts, depending on population. The state constitution was adopted in 1793. In addition to its two U.S. senators, Vermont has one representative in the U.S.

House of Representatives. The state has three votes in the electoral college.

The first Tuesday in March is Town Meeting Day. The tradition of the March town meeting began in the colonial period and continues today.

Sports
Vermont's major sport is skiing and there are many areas devoted to this activity including Bromley, Stratton, Stowe and Sugarbush. Hunting and fishing are popular in other seasons. There are 47 cross-country and 24 alpine ski areas in Vermont. Hunting, fishing, camping, and hiking are popular in other seasons.

Major Cities
Barre (population 9,482). Settled in 1793 as Wildersburgh, the name was changed to Barre later that year. Barre is known as the center of Vermont's granite quarrying regions. In the early 1800s, immigrant

The Shelburne Museum, outside of Burlington, was founded by Electra Havemeyer Webb to "show the craftsmanship and ingenuity of our forebears." The historic lighthouse below and the paddlewheeler S.S. Ticonderoga at left are part of the museum's vast collection of Americana relating to this country's history, culture, and art.

Bicycle touring through the scenic Vermont countryside has grown in popularity in recent years.

laborers flocked to Barre to get jobs in the quarries. Visitors can tour the Rock of Ages granite quarry and observe the craftsmen at work. The Hope Cemetery is one of the largest displays of Barre's granite and other fine sculptures can be found throughout the city.

Bennington (population 16,451). Settled in 1761, Bennington was the headquarters for Ethan

Allen's Green Mountain Boys. On August 16, 1777, one of the most decisive battles of the Revolution was fought near here by these same Green Mountain Boys. Downtown Bennington is listed on the National Register of Historic Places. Travelers may visit the Park-McCullough House (1865), the Bennington Battle Monument, the Bennington Museum, the Old First Church (1805), and the

Hawkins House Crafts Gallery (1807).

Burlington (population 39,127). Settled in 1773, Burlington is the largest city in Vermont. It is also the site of the oldest university (the University of Vermont, founded in 1791) and the oldest daily newspaper (1848) in the state. There are some 72 industries in Burlington. Travelers may visit the Discovery Museum, Robert Hull Fleming Museum, Shelburne Museum, Shelburne Farms, the Vermont Wildflower Farm, Battery Park, and the Green Mountain Audubon Nature Center.

Montpelier (population 8,247). Settled in 1787, Montpelier is the capital of the state and is located on the banks of the Winooski River. Places to visit include the State House (1859), the Vermont Historical Society and Museum, the Thomas Waterman Wood Art Gallery, the Kent Tavern Museum (1837), and the

Morse Farm Sugar Shack.

Places To Visit

The National Park Service maintains the 270,000 acres that comprise the Green Mountain National Forest in Vermont. In addition, there are 36 state recreation areas.

Arlington: Candle Mill Village. The village contains three old buildings, one of them a gristmill, dating back to 1764..

Bellows Falls: Green Mountain Railroad. Visitors can take a train ride through three beautiful valleys.

Brandon: Stephen A. Douglas Birthplace. This is the cottage where "The Little Giant," the statesman famous for his debates with Abraham Lincoln, was born in 1813.

Brattleboro: Creamery Bridge. Here is one of Vermont's best-preserved covered bridges.

Grafton: The Old Tavern. Built in 1801, this tavern is still a working inn.

Ludlow: Crowley Cheese Factory. In this cheese factory, the oldest one in the United States, cheese is still made by hand.

The University of Vermont in central Burlington is the state's oldest university.

Manchester Village: Historic Hildene. This house, built in 1904, was the home of Robert Todd Lincoln, son of President Abraham Lincoln. The Southern Vermont Art Center.

Middlebury: UVM Morgan Horse Farm. The University of Vermont maintains a breeding and training farm for the Morgan horses.

Plymouth Notch: President Calvin Coolidge Homestead. It was here that the 30th President was sworn in by his father in 1923.

Quechee: Quechee Gorge was carved out by a glacier and river and boasts a 165-foot drop to the bottom.

Rutland: Norman Rockwell Museum. This is a collection of more than 2,000 pictures and memorabilia of the late artist.

Saint Albans: Chester A. Arthur Historic Site. Here is a replica of the second home of our 21st President.

Saint Johnsbury: St. Johnsbury Athenaeum, the Maple Grove Maple Museum, and the Fairbanks Museum and Planetarium

Shelburne: Shelburne Museum. Many historic buildings as well as the paddle wheeler S.S. *Ticonderoga*, a lighthouse, and a covered bridge are situated in this 45-acre park, which has been called the best collection of Americana in New England.

South Hero: Hyde Log Cabin. Much of this restored cabin came from the original dwelling, built in 1783.

South Strafford: Justin Morril Homestead. This homestead is thought by

Hildene, a historic estate in Manchester, once belonged to Robert Todd Lincoln, the son of President Abraham Lincoln.

The Hyde Log Cabin, built in 1783, is considered the nation's oldest log cabin standing on its original foundations.

some to be the finest Gothic Revival house in Vermont, and was once the home of the statesman whose name it bears.

Springfield: Eureka Schoolhouse. This schoolhouse, the oldest in Vermont, was built in 1790.

Stowe: Bloody Brook School House. Here is a restored one-room school that was originally built around 1880.

Sunderland: The homes of Ira and Ethan Allen

Waterbury: Cold Hollow Cider Mill. Cider from local apples is produced here, and samples are served. Ben & Jerry's ice cream factory.

Windsor: Constitution House. It was in this 18th-century tavern that the constitution of New Connecticut was signed in 1777.

Woodstock: Billings Farm and Museum. This is a working dairy farm that is about 100 years old. Demonstrations of period farm activities are given here. Just outside of town is the Raptor Center of the Vermont Institute of Natural Science.

Events

There are many events and organizations that schedule activities of various kinds in the state of Vermont. Here are some of them.

Sports: Greyhound racing at Green Mountain Race Track (Bennington), Winter Carnival (Brattleboro), Vermont State Open Golf Tournament (Fairlee), Killington Mountain Equestrian Festival (Killington), Winter Carnival (Middlebury).

Arts and Crafts: Antique and Classic Car Show (Bennington), Antique Show (Bennington), Addison County Home and Garden Show (Middlebury), Fall Festival of Vermont Crafts (Montpelier), Vermont Quilt Festival (Northfield), Stratton Arts Festival (Stratton Mountain), Mount Snow Foliage Craft Fair (West Dover).

Music: Old Time Fiddlers' Contest (Barre), Certified Vermont State Championship Fiddlers' Contest (Bellows Falls), Yellow Barn Music Festival (Brattleboro), band concerts (Burlington), Vermont Mozart Festival (Burlington), Marlboro Music Festival (Marlboro), St. Johnsbury Town Band (St. Johnsbury).

Entertainment: Rockingham Old Home Days (Bellows Falls), Lake Champlain Discovery Festival (Burlington), Lobster Festival (Fairlee), Festival on the Green (Middlebury), Labor Day Festival (Northfield), Vermont State Fair (Rutland), Maple Sugar Festival (Saint Albans), Bay Day (Saint Albans), Lake Champlain Balloon Festival (Shelburne), Wurstfest (Stratton Mountain), Deerfield Valley Farmers Day Exhibition (Wilmington).

Tours: Rock of Ages Quarry and Craftsman Center (Barre), Bennington Potters, Inc. (Bennington).

Theater: Saint Michael's Playhouse (Burlington), Champlain Shakespeare Festival (Burlington), Dorset Theatre Festival (Dorset), Weston Playhouse (Weston).

North Ferrisburg, in northwestern Vermont, is part of the Champlain Valley. This area, on the banks of Lake Champlain, has some of the state's best farmland.

The Land

Vermont is bounded on the west by New York, on the north by the Canadian province of Quebec, on the east by New Hampshire, and on the south by Massachusetts. The state has six main land regions: the White Mountains, the Western New England Upland, the Green Mountains, the Vermont Valley, the Taconic Mountains, and the Champlain Valley.

The White Mountain Region is in the northeastern part of the state; Vermont shares these mountains with New Hampshire and Maine. The White Mountains include peaks that rise more than 3,000 feet, with many swift-running streams flowing between them. Potatoes are grown here, but the region is too hilly for extensive farming.

Northeastern Vermont contains high peaks and rocky lands nourished by swift rivers and streams. Some vegetables are grown here, but the region is too rugged for extensive farming.

The Western New England Upland comprises most of Vermont's eastern border area and extends into Massachusetts and Connecticut. It is sometimes called the Vermont Piedmont. The region has broad, fertile lowlands where dairy cattle graze and apples and strawberries thrive. The western section has granite hills and quarries and forests that produce timber for lumber and paper products.

Vermont contains some of the largest granite quarries in the world. The Vermont Valley is also renowned for its fine white marble; near the New York border, excellent slate can be found.

Waitsfield, in north-central Vermont, is in the Green Mountain region. Beef cattle and maple syrup are among the agricultural products of this area.

The tree-covered Green Mountains, which give Vermont its nickname of Green Mountain State, range from the northern to the southern border in central Vermont. Oats, beef cattle, and maple syrup are produced here, and tourism is a major industry. Mount Mansfield, the highest point in the state at 4,393 feet, is in the Green Mountains.

Farms dot the tree-covered landscape of central Vermont, where the land supports beef, dairy, and fruit farms.

The Vermont Valley is a narrow strip of land located in the southwestern part of the state and extending about halfway up Vermont. This is dairy, fruit, maple-syrup, and forest-products country.

The Taconic Mountains rise more than 3,000 feet in southwestern Vermont and extend into Massachusetts. They have many swift-running streams and overlook tranquil lakes of unspoiled beauty. Some poultry is raised here, and potatoes are farmed.

The Champlain Valley, also called the Vermont Lowland, consists of a narrow strip in the northwestern part of the state that includes some of Vermont's best farmland. Dairy cattle are raised here, and farmers grow oats, potatoes, corn, hay, and fruit.

Vermont's winters are long: snow arrives before Christmas and lasts at least until early April. Some 64 inches of snow fall each year in southern Vermont, and accumulations may reach more than 82 inches in the mountainous northern regions.

Approximately 75 percent of Vermont's trees are hardwood, including maple, birch, basswood, and poplar. Farmers tapping the maple trees for syrup are a common sight during the late winter months.

The most important rivers of Vermont are the Connecticut, the Batten Kill, the Missisquoi, the Lamoille, the Winooski, and Otter Creek—the state's longest river. There are some 430 lakes and ponds in Vermont, most of them in the Northeast. Lake Memphremagog is the largest lake completely inside the state's borders. Lake Champlai covering 490 square miles, is the largest in New England and forms part of the border between Vermont and New York. The lake, whicl was linked to the Hudson River by a canal, provided an important port for the state's goods.

The Climate

Vermont's climate is humid, with an annual precipitation of 35 to 45 inches. Much of this is in the form of snow, which may reach 120 inches in the Green Mountains. Winters are long and cold, with temperatures sometimes falling below 0 degrees Fahrenheit. Summers are cool and sunny. Rutland, in southern Vermont, has an average January temperature of about 20 degrees Fahrenheit; the July average is 70 degrees F. In Burlington, to the north, the January average is about 18 degrees F. and the July average 68 degrees F.

The History

Present-day Vermont was originally populated by Indians of the Abnaki, Mahican, and Pennacook tribes of the Algonquian language family. These tribes were hunters and farmers, whom invading Iroquois, from what is now New York State, drove out before the explorers came. They returned in the early 1600s, when the French helped them defeat the Iroquois.

In 1609 Frenchman Samuel de Champlain explored the large lake later named for him and claimed the Vermont region for France. In 1666 the French built a fort on Isle La Motte in Lake Champlain, south of their Canadian holdings, and in 1690 British soldiers from Albany, New York, established a fort at Chimney Point, near present-day Middlebury. The stage was set for decades of struggle between French and British claimants to the region. During the French and Indian Wars, which ended in 1763 in a British victory, the Lake Champlain region was a major battleground between the British and the French and their Indian allies.

Vermont was the last New England state to be settled, beginning in

Ethan Allen led Vermont's Green Mountain Boys in their fight to defend the region's land from settlement by New Yorkers. After the American Revolution began, Allen and his men joined forces with General Benedict Arnold to capture Fort Ticonderoga from the British on May 10, 1775.

1742, when Fort Drummer was built at what is now Brattleboro by Massachusetts settlers protecting their colony's western frontier. Vermont land was also disputed among neighboring colonies between 1749 and 1770. The royal governor of New Hampshire made over 100 grants of Vermont land that was also claimed by New York, and settlers from both states moved in. The British government recognized the New York claim in 1764, ordering settlers who held New Hampshire Grants to give up their land or buy it from New York. This unpopular decision angered many settlers, and in 1770 a dissident military force called the Green Mountain Boys attacked New York settlers and drove them from Vermont.

When the Revolutionary War began in 1775, Vermonters united to back the rebellious colonists. Ethan Allen, Benedict Arnold, and more than 80 of the Green Mountain Boys made Vermont famous when they took Fort Ticonderoga from the British in 1775. Colonial troops occupied the fort until 1777, when they were driven out by the British. At the Battle of Bennington, fought in New York, just west of Vermont, on August 16, 1777, the British suffered a defeat that helped alter the course of the war.

Early in 1777, weary of arguments with New Hampshire and New York, Vermont settlers declared their region an independent republic, which they called New Connecticut. Six months later they adopted the name Vermont (from the French *Vert Mont*, or Green Mountain). They also drafted a state constitution which was unique in prohibiting human slavery and granting all males the right to vote, regardless of their property or income.

But Vermont's problems were not over. New Hampshire and New York still claimed parts of the republic. In 1783, when the Revolutionary War ended, George Washington considered sending troops to overthrow the Vermont government, but decided against it. Vermont remained an independent republic for 14 years, running its own postal service, coining its own money, naturalizing citizens of other states and countries, and negotiating with other states and nations. In 1790 New Hampshire finally gave up its claim to Vermont, and Vermont paid New York $30,000 for disputed territory. This cleared the way for Vermont to enter the Union in 1791 as the 14th state.

Many Vermont men fought in the War of 1812 with Great Britain, although the conflict was unpopular because Vermont had a great deal of trade with British Canada. After the war, the newly opened Champlain Canal, which connected the lake and New York's Hudson River, gave Vermont farmers a way to ship their goods south and rendered trade with Canada less important. Farmers prospered, and sheep raising became a big industry. When wool prices dropped in the mid-1800s, Vermont shifted to dairy farming.

Some 34,000 Vermont men served with Union forces during the Civil War, which began in 1861. And the war's northernmost action was fought in the state, when a group of 22 Confederate soldiers robbed banks in St. Albans and escaped to Canada with more than $20,000.

Although agriculture declined in Vermont after the Civil War ended in 1865, industry began to prosper, especially wood processing and cheese-making. Burlington became an important lumber port, and Barre was the center of a booming granite industry that supplied cut stone for buildings and monuments. Valuable marble deposits around Proctor and Rutland were quarried. By the early 1900s, Vermont was becoming more of a manufacturing than a farming state. Vermont lumber and machinery were important to the armed forces during World War I, which the United States entered in 1917.

During the Great Depression of the 1930s, many Vermont factories and mills closed, some of them permanently. Small farms declined, and the trend toward larger farms would continue after economic recovery. When the United States entered World War II in 1941, Vermont factories increased their output of lumber, machinery, and other products, although the textile industry was adversely affected by Southern competition, as in other New England states.

Today Vermont is still growing economically. Major corporations have built factories in the state, and the tourist industry prospers in both summer and winter. The large resort hotels and vacation camps of the early 20th century have been joined by more than 56 ski areas

Joseph Smith, a native of Sharon, Vermont, founded the Church of Jesus Christ of Latter-day Saints—the Mormon Church—in 1830. This faith was born at a time when several other religious groups, including the Millerites and the Perfectionists, originated in northern New England. During the 1820s and 1830s, these communities, with their radically new interpretations of the Bible, won many converts despite strong opposition from those who did not share their beliefs.

Montpelier, the state capital, is Vermont's third largest city. In recent years it has prospered from a year-round surge in tourism.

that attract many visitors, especially the Green Mountains. Vermont has been at the forefront of environmental conservation. In the 1990s, a stringent water quality law was enacted and land speculation has been limited.

Education

The first free public school in Vermont opened in Guilford in 1761, and the Vermont constitution of 1777 required that each town have a public school. The first secondary school was established in Bennington in 1780. In 1823, Samuel R. Hall founded in Concord the first U.S. school to focus on teacher training. Vermont's first institution of higher education was the University of Vermont, founded in 1791. Middlebury College (1800) and Norwich University (1819) soon followed. Today the state has nine colleges and universities.

The People

Almost 34 percent of the people in Vermont live in towns and cities, including Burlington, Rutland, Barre, and Montpelier. Most of them were born in the United States, and more than half of those born elsewhere came from Canada. The largest religious group in the state consists of Roman Catholics. Other large denominations are the United Church of Christ, Methodists, Baptists, and Episcopalians.

Thaddeus Stevens, born in the frontier village of Danville, was a prominent politician during the Civil War and Reconstruction eras. Stevens opposed slavery and fought bitterly against any compromise with the South during the crisis of 1860–61, which culminated in the Civil War.

Chester A. Arthur, the 21st president of the United States, was born in Fairfield, Vermont.

Robert Frost, best known for his poems about rural New England, won the Pulitzer Prize for poetry in 1924, 1931, 1937, and 1943. In January 1961 he read one of his poems at the inauguration of President Kennedy.

Calvin Coolidge, a native of Plymouth Notch, was America's 30th president. He succeeded President Warren G. Harding, who died in office in 1923. During his six years in the White House, Coolidge improved relations with Mexico and supported American business at home and abroad.

Famous People

Many famous people were born in the state of Vermont. Here are a few:

Artist
Richard Morris Hunt 1827-95, Brattleboro. Architect

Philosophers and Religious Leaders
John Dewey 1859-1952, Burlington. Educational philosopher

William Chauncey Langdon 1831-95, Burlington. Episcopal clergyman and cofounder of the YMCA

Joseph Smith 1805-44, Sharon. Founder of the Church of Jesus Christ of the Latter Day Saints (Mormons)

Brigham Young 1801-77, Whitingham. Leader of the westward Mormon migration

Government Officials
Chester Alan Arthur 1829-86, Fairfield. Twenty-first President of the United States

Calvin Coolidge 1872-1933, Plymouth. Thirteenth President of the United States

Stephen A. Douglas 1813-61, Brandon. U.S. senator and famed orator

Business Leaders
James Fisk 1834-72, Bennington. Financier who made $11 million as a result of Black Friday in 1869

Stephen Douglas is best known for his series of debates with Lincoln before the Civil War.

Henry M. Leland 1843-1932, Danville. President of the Cadillac Motor Company and the Lincoln Motor Company

Robert G. Letourneau 1888-1969, Richford. Heavy equipment manufacturer

William H. Russell 1812-72, Burlington. Founder of the Pony Express

Henry W. Wells 1805-78, Thetford. President of American Express, partner of Wells, Fargo and Co.

Daniel Willard 1861-1942, North Hartland. President of the Baltimore & Ohio Railroad

Social Reformers
Robert H. Smith 1879-1950, Saint Johnsbury. Cofounder of Alcoholics Anonymous

William G. Wilson 1895-1971, East Dorset. Cofounder of Alcoholics Anonymous

Inventor
John Deere 1804-86, Rutland.

George Dewey commanded the U.S. fleet which defeated the Spanish in the Battle of Manila Bay in 1898.

Inventor of the first steel plow
Elisha Otis 1811-61, Halifax. Invented first safety elevator

Naval Figure
George Dewey 1837-1917, Montpelier. Admiral in the Spanish-American War

Colleges and Universities
There are a number of colleges and universities in Vermont. Here are the most prominent, with their locations, dates of founding, and enrollment.
Bennington College, Bennington, 1932, 510
Castleton State College, Castleton, 1787, 2,028
Goddard College, Plainfield, 1938, 363
Johnson State College, Johnson, 1828, 1,758
Middlebury College, Middlebury, 1800, 1,960
Norwich University, Northfield, 1819, 2,620

William Wilson was the co-founder of Alcoholics Anonymous in 1935.

Saint Michael's College, Winooski, 1904, 2,555
Trinity College, Burlington, 1925, 1,115
University of Vermont, Burlington, 1791, 9,532

Where To Get More Information
Vermont Travel Division
134 State Street
Montpelier, VT 05602

Further Reading

General

Aylesworth, Thomas G., and Virginia L. Aylesworth. *Let's Discover the States: Northern New England.* New York: Chelsea House Publishers, 1988.

Maine

Bailey, Bernadine. *Picture Book of Maine,* rev. ed. Chicago: Whitman, 1967.

Berchen, William. *Maine.* Boston: Houghton Mifflin, 1973.

Carpenter, Allan. *Maine,* rev. ed. Chicago: Childrens Press, 1979.

Clark, Charles E. *Maine: A Bicentennial History.* New York: Norton, 1977.

Clark, Charles E. *Maine, a History.* New York: Norton, 1985.

Harrington, Ty. *America the Beautiful: Maine.* Chicago: Childrens Press, 1989.

Williamson, William D. *The History of the State of Maine.* 2 vols. Freeport, Maine: Cumberland Press, 1966.

New Hampshire

Bailey, Bernadine. *Picture Book of New Hampshire,* rev. ed. Chicago: Whitman, 1971.

Carpenter, Allen. *New Hampshire,* rev. ed. Chicago: Childrens Press, 1979.

Fradin, Dennis B. *From Sea to Shining Sea: New Hampshire.* Chicago: Childrens Press, 1992.

Jager, Ronald, and Grace Jager. *New Hampshire, an Illustrated History of the Granite State.* Woodland Hills, California: Windsor Publications, 1983.

McNair, Sylvia. *America the Beautiful: New Hampshire.* Chicago: Childrens Press, 1992.

Morison, Elting E., and Elizabeth F. Morison. *New Hampshire: A Bicentennial History.* New York: Norton, 1976.

Morison, Elizabeth F., and Elting E. Morison. *New Hampshire, a History.* New York: Norton, 1985.

Vermont

Carpenter, Allan. *Vermont,* rev. ed. Chicago: Childrens Press, 1979.

Cheney, Cora. *Vermont: The State with the Storybook Past.* Brattleboro, Vermont: Stephen Green Press, 1976.

Fradin, Dennis B. *From Sea to Shining Sea: Vermont.* Chicago: Childrens Press, 1993.

McNair, Sylvia. *America the Beautiful: Vermont.* Chicago: Childrens Press, 1991.

Morissey, Charles T. *Vermont: A Bicentennial History.* New York: Norton, 1980.

Morissey, Charles T. *Vermont, a History.* New York: Norton, 1984.

Numbers in italic refer to illustrations

Picture Credits

AP/Wide World Photos: pp. 32, 33, 60, 61, 92, 93; J. Northrup Bennet: p. 57 (right); David Brownell: p. 50 (right); Courtesy of Joseph Devenney/Maine Office of Tourism: pp. 3 (top), 9, 20, 22; Richard Glassman: pp. 6-7, 13, 28, 56; William Johnson: p. 50 (left); James Kersell: pp. 10, 40, 41, 68 (top); Library of Congress: pp. 24, 26, 84, 91 (right); Courtesy of Maine Office of Tourism: pp. 11, 12, 14, 15, 16, 17, 18, 19; National Portrait Gallery: pp. 29, 30, 31, 53, 58, 59, 87, 89, 90, 91 (left); Courtesy of New Hampshire Office of Vacation Travel: pp. 36-37, 42, 43, 44, 45, 49, 54, 57 (left); M. T. Pinkerton: pp. 3 (bottom), 46-47, 48; Stokes Collection, New York Public Library: p. 55; Vermont Travel Division: pp. 4, 64-65, 67, 68 (bottom), 69, 70, 71, 72, 73, 74, 75, 76, 77, 78, 79, 80, 81, 82, 88.

Cover photos courtesy of Maine Office of Tourism and Vermont Travel Division.